To

_____

From

_____

Date

_____

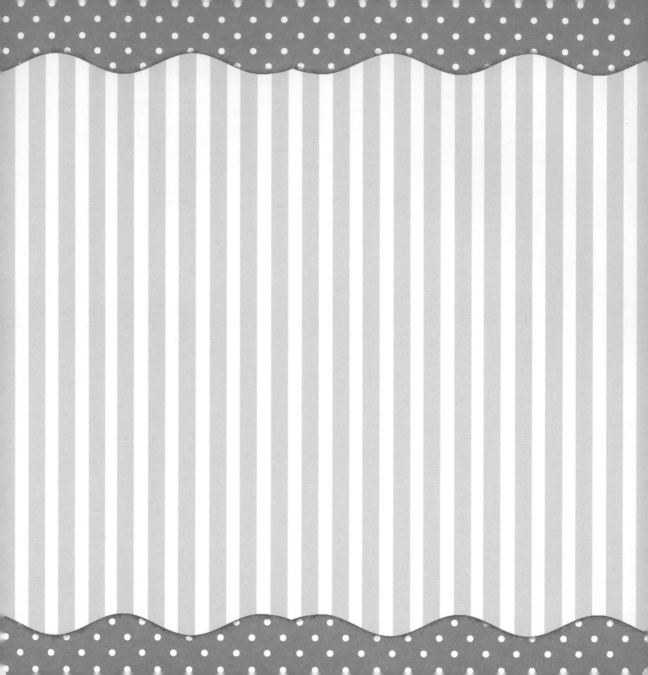

As Grandma Says

Judith Robl

ARTWORK BY

Audrey Jeanne Roberts

HARVEST HOUSE PUBLISHERS

EUGENE, OREGON

As Grandma Says

Text copyright © 2011 by Judith Robl
Illustrations copyright © 2011 by Audrey Jeanne Roberts
Published by Harvest House Publishers
Eugene, Oregon 97402
www.harvesthousepublishers.com

ISBN: 978-0-7369-3004-8

My thanks to Judith Robl for writing such a delightful book. It brought wonderful memories of my own grandmothers and the wisdom they so graciously shared. My Grandma Heyser, whom we called "Nanny," and Grandma Flint are both now with the Lord. These two women were two of the most precious gifts God ever gave me.

– Audrey Jeanne Roberts

IN MEMORY OF
Lucille Bigler,
the grandmother who taught me;

Sandra Clarke,
the sister-in-Christ who loved me; and

Jim Steinert,
the brother-in-Christ who believed in me.

– Judith Robl

Grandma's Wisdom

As the Twig Is Bent So Grows the Tree

When we moved into our current home, there were large maple trees at the front of the lot. Along the driveway behind one of the maples someone had planted a walnut tree too close to the maple in front of it. As the walnut tree grew, it leaned away from the maple so it could get more sunlight. After we removed the maple because of age and disease, the walnut tree still leaned. While it was a young sapling, it could have been staked and made to grow straight. But by the time the maple tree was removed, the walnut's form was fixed. Years of growth in that slanted direction made it inflexible. Its leaning habit was uncorrectable.

Children are much like that sapling. While they are young, we have the ability to direct their growth. We can inculcate good habits of hygiene, neatness, respect, and obedience. But we need to begin early. When they try to bend the rules, and they will, we need to bring them back into compliance. This need not be done by force, but by reason and reward.

Train a child in the way he should go, and when he is old he will not turn from it (Proverbs 22:6).

Seeing children grow up well and establish families of their own is the grand reward of parenting. Our job is to bend the twig and let the Lord direct the growing.

Father God, make me equal to the task of tending the children You entrust to me. Help me instill in them reverence and respect for You so they will love and trust You. In Jesus' most precious name. Amen.

Beauty Is Only Skin Deep

My grandma always said that you can't take credit for whether you are beautiful or not. Face and form are gifts from God. He decides on your looks. That isn't to say that looks are not important. Every woman should take care of her appearance because the outside of a person draws the interest of casual observers and makes them want to know her better.

Before she was presented to the king, Esther spent a year in the house of the women, taking care of her body with creams and perfumes. Her skin was soft and suffused with sweet aromas. Her appearance pleased the king.

> When the turn came for Esther...to go to the king, she asked for nothing other than what Hegai, the king's eunuch who was in charge of the harem, suggested. *And Esther won the favor of everyone who saw her* (Esther 2:15).

Esther's true beauty, however, lay in her fidelity to her people, her reverent spirit, and her willingness to lay her life on the line for what she believed. Creams and powders and diet and exercise are critical to the upkeep of our bodies, but they should never become the main focus of our attention. Things of the spirit are more important.

Father God, *help me remember that while appearance is important, it is not everything. Keep me focused on things of eternal value. In Jesus' most precious name. Amen.*

Because I Said So

When my grandmother issued instructions, she didn't allow for argument. When asked why about something, her answer was always, "Because I said so." She never explained. She assumed we would know her dictates were meant for our good or the benefit of the family; therefore, they were to be carried out.

The spoken word carries great power. If we look at the book of Genesis, we see that in the beginning "God said" and it was so. He didn't explain or persuade or cajole. "He said" and "it was." Period.

When my children were small and the inevitable "why" question arose, I tried to answer informatively. They had more whys than I had answers though. My final answer was usually, "If I knew that, I'd be as smart as God. And nobody is as smart as God."

There are times when we want to know the why of things. Why did the business fail? Why was this young person taken in the flower of life? Why did a friend get cancer? Why won't my children listen to me? Why can't I make a consistently good pie crust? Our whys run the gamut from the serious to the sublimely ridiculous. And still we ask. But the truth is...

God said, "Let there be light," and there was light (Genesis 1:3).

God had a plan—and He still has a plan. He doesn't have to divulge that plan to us. Our part is to be available and ready because He tells us to be.

Father God, help me keep my faith in You when Your plan seems mysterious. Help me be faithfully obedient even when I can't see the reason why for something. In Jesus' most precious name. Amen.

Better to Remain Silent and Be Thought a Fool Than to Open Your Mouth and Remove All Doubt

People love to talk. Unfortunately, when we talk a lot, our tongues frequently run faster than our wits. That's when the trouble starts. Often we seem to need to keep talking to prove how much we know, to impress others with our vocabulary, and to reassure ourselves that we are important. This often has the opposite effect by revealing our shortcomings, resulting in our feeling much smaller and more insignificant. Worse yet, in the heat of a discussion, we sometimes say things that are hurtful or mean.

Once spoken, words cannot be recalled. Look at some of our terms for people who talk too much: fast-talking salesman, inveterate gossip, harpy, nag. None of these conjure up a vision of someone we would trust implicitly. We tend to avoid these people.

> A man of knowledge uses words with restraint, and a man of understanding is even-tempered. Even a fool is thought wise if he keeps silent, and discerning if he holds his tongue (Proverbs 17:27-28).

The wisest people I know are the most reserved as well. They don't push their opinions on others, although they'll answer questions. They never engage in gossip, and it's impossible to draw them into arguments. When they speak, they have something valuable to contribute to the conversation.

Father God, *You give wisdom to those who ask. Keep me silent in the places where I need to be silent and give me Your words when I am required to speak. In Jesus' most precious name. Amen.*

A Clear Conscience Is a Soft Pillow, and Confession Is Good for the Soul

My first job was as a summer wheat agent for the local railroad. I did the office work for a station that was open from June 15 to August 15 to accommodate the local grain elevator. The auditor who checked me in said, "I don't care if you have 20 dollars worth of business or 20,000 dollars worth of business, your books *will* balance to the penny." And he taught me how to keep accounts accurately. The basic principle was to enter each transaction immediately—not ten minutes later. The corollary to that principle was to enter the transaction accurately. The final part was to double-check my work.

I've discovered these principles work well when keeping accounts with God too. When I transgress, I own up as soon as I realize it. I don't wait for Sunday service or tomorrow's quiet time. *Now* is the hour when I bring it to God and agree with Him that it was wrong. I define the sin accurately, without excuses or casting blame on others. Then I resolve to change that habit and take the first steps toward doing so.

In vain you rise early and stay up late, toiling for food to eat—for he grants sleep to those he loves (Psalm 127:2).

When I deliberately hide a sin, I've taken myself out of fellowship with God. When I confess my sin, He restores me to fellowship and I enjoy the full benefits of being His child.

Father God, *quicken my spirit to be sensitive to my trespasses. Make me willing and eager to bring them to You in confession and repentance. In Jesus' most precious name. Amen.*

Cutting a Wide Peel from a Small Potato

Until I had a home of my own and potatoes to peel for meals, I didn't quite get the gist of my grandmother's criticism of one of our neighbors: "She cuts a wide peel from a small potato." This lady lived in a small house that she had decorated lavishly. She dressed in the height of fashion. Her hair and makeup were always flawless. She carried an air of elegance wherever she went. Her husband was a modest man whose wages could barely support her extravagances. They could never seem to get ahead financially. Eventually debt lost them their house.

> In the house of the wise are stores of choice food and oil, but a foolish man devours all he has (Proverbs 21:20).

When you have a small potato, you peel very thin, slender strips so you don't lose much potato with the peeling. As a young wife and mother, I became very conscious of the waste incurred while cutting a wide peel from a small potato. Then it dawned on me that cutting a wide peel from a large potato was just as wasteful, but it wasn't so obvious.

Wisdom includes living within our means, whether large or small, and storing resources for the future. And a large income doesn't give us leave to live extravagantly. If we live modestly, even on a small income, we can help others too.

Father God, grant me the wisdom to live wisely, reflecting Your values in every facet of my life and purse. In Jesus' most precious name. Amen.

Do Not Ostracize the Sawbuck and Expect Things to Turn Out like Grandma Used to Make

The sawbuck referred to here is not a ten-dollar bill. It is an X-shaped framework that holds wood for cutting with a handsaw. Sawing in this fashion requires diligent, sweaty effort. You need to put your whole being into the project. Your legs and back work as hard as your arm and hand holding the saw. It is a perfect picture of long, hard work.

Our grandmothers engaged in long, hard work. Keeping house, making meals, and rearing children were done without the modern conveniences we have today. Homemade bread didn't come out of a bread machine. It was kneaded by hand on a floured board, set to rise, punched down, and kneaded again. That took much more effort than putting the ingredients into a machine and walking off. And the resulting bread was very different in texture from what comes out of today's machines.

There is no substitute for physical work when acquiring those things we desire. Work not only gets things done, it builds discipline and dedication and provides accomplishments.

> The sluggard craves and gets nothing, but the desires of the diligent are fully satisfied (Proverbs 13:4).

Baking bread gives off a tantalizing aroma. We notice it each time we drive past a bakery. But that aroma is much more satisfying when it rises from our own kitchens!

Father God, help me value the process of work and not just the results. Grant me the wisdom to see it as training for Your service. In Jesus' most precious name. Amen.

Don't Burn Your Bridges
Before You Cross Them

The original adage was about burning bridges behind you. It generally referred to something said or done that damaged or destroyed a relationship. My grandmother, however, appropriated that metaphor for self-limiting behaviors and thoughts. To her, burning your bridge before you cross indicated that you had discarded a possibility without giving it due consideration.

We all say things like "I'm too old to take up skydiving" or "I'll never learn to dance because I'm too clumsy." When we tell ourselves such things, we limit ourselves to the status quo. When God called Moses to lead the children of Israel out of their Egyptian captivity, Moses demurred. He told God the people wouldn't believe him. So God gave him the rod that turned into a serpent, let Moses' hand turn leprous and back again on command, and allowed him to turn some Nile water into blood as signs to convince the people. Then Moses complained that he couldn't speak well, so God gave him Aaron as a spokesman to the people (Exodus 4). *God is not limited.* And He doesn't intend for us to be limited either. We are to be able to say with Paul,

> I can do everything through him who gives me strength (Philippians 4:13).

As long as we are in Christ, doing what He would have us do, He will give us the strength and ability to complete the tasks He sets before us.

Father God, strengthen my resolve to be faithful to the tasks You have set before me, no matter how inadequate I feel. Remind me that You are my strength. In Jesus' most precious name. Amen.

Don't Cut Off Your Nose to Spite Your Face

At first glance, "don't cut off your nose to spite your face" seems to make no sense. Who would cut off their own nose? Nobody, of course. But we can do it mentally or emotionally. Our irritations and angers can be ridiculously destructive if we let them go. Anger is corrosive and eats away at whoever holds it.

Grandma had no patience with spats and grudges. She felt that time could be better spent in activities other than trying to think up ways to get even. She taught me that I can choose to be angry or choose not to be. I get to decide. Here's a great example.

Two sisters had a falling out. It wasn't over something inconsequential; it involved a life-changing event. They each handled it differently, and neither could see the other's point of view. For 20 years they didn't speak. If one was at a family gathering, the other stayed away. Finally the first sister offered an olive branch and the other accepted. They went to a ladies' meeting together at the eldest sister's church and heard a teaching on forgiveness. At last report they were talking about the incident that had caused the rift and still attending family functions together. But the grief they had caused the family couldn't be taken back, and they had lost 20 years of fellowship with one another.

> Do not be quickly provoked in your spirit, for anger resides in the lap of fools (Ecclesiastes 7:9).

No matter the provocation, holding on to anger robs us, not just the persons with whom we are angry. Why should we let anyone else have that much control over our lives?

Father God, help me release those who offend me into Your capable hands. Give me the grace to forgive—and not just for their sakes, but for mine too. In Jesus' most precious name. Amen.

Experience Is a Dear School, but a Fool Will Learn in No Other

My grandmother had little patience for people who would not learn. She often said she was never disciplined twice for the same offense. Then she added it was a marvel how many new ways she thought of to get into trouble!

Nothing has tempted us or happened to us that is not common to all people. We all have the same needs for physical well-being. We all have personal desires and ambitions. They may be different in detail for each person, but they are similar nonetheless.

Our culture today thinks the world is different now than what it used to be. Things that are "old school" seem to have no relevance. But even though technology has advanced, the nature of mankind hasn't changed. We may be fighting with high-tech weapons in battles broadcast live instead of using spears and swords with runners bringing the news of battle days later, but the reasons for war are the same as they have always been. Greed, jealousy, and lust for control still fuel most conflicts.

And disobedience to God's Word still has consequences. Truth never changes. Details change, but the principle remains the same.

> A fool spurns his father's discipline, but whoever heeds correction shows prudence (Proverbs 15:5).

Learning life's lessons is not optional, but we can influence our methods of instruction. The trial-and-error method is effective, but inefficient and costly. Learning from others is much less expensive and time-consuming.

Father God, save me from the arrogance that says no one else has gone through the same problems I am facing today. Grant me the grace to learn willingly from those with more experience. In Jesus' most precious name. Amen.

Give Generously from Your Own Purse

My grandmother lived her entire life within financial limitations. That did not keep her from charitable efforts. Her industry and thrift provided the means to give. Her garden yielded vegetables that she canned and preserved for use during the fall and winter. Her chicken house provided eggs as well as meat. The apple, peach, and pear trees on the property gave us fruit in season and jams for the future. I can still taste her pear honey.

When Elijah went to Zarephath, he asked a widow there for food and water. He knew God intended for her to provide for him. She didn't know that, but she gave as he asked. Her generosity in the midst of her own need is our good example.

> "As surely as the LORD your God lives," she replied, "I don't have any bread—only a handful of flour in a jar and a little oil in a jug. I am gathering a few sticks to take home and make a meal for myself and my son, that we may eat it—and die." Elijah said to her, "Don't be afraid. Go home and do as you have said. But first make a small cake of bread for me from what you have and bring it to me, and then make something for yourself and your son"
> (1 Kings 17:12-13).

Note that she didn't go to a neighbor to ask for help. She provided what she had, and the Lord increased it to feed His prophet, the widow, and the widow's son for a long time. If we give God what we have, He will do wonders with our offerings of faith.

Father God, *teach me to be generous even in my want. Grant me the grace to rely on Your provision, especially when I can't see how I'm going to get something I need to do accomplished. In Jesus' most precious name. Amen.*

The Heart Matters

My grandmother was not impressed by appearances. Oh, appearances mattered to some degree, but only so far as it made you presentable in polite company. Clean and neat were expected. Pleasant and smiling were required. Appropriate garb and ladylike deportment were demanded. Beyond those, appearances held little importance.

I remembered this lesson when my son carried boxes and bags at our local grocery. There was an older, middle-aged lady who came in several times a day. Her dress was modest, but the accessories didn't always match. Her hair was clean, but not coiffed. When my son came to me one day asking about this strange woman, I was able to steer him into looking *beyond* her outward appearance to see her heart.

I explained this older lady worked for elderly and housebound people, tending their homes, buying their groceries, and praying for them. Her soft voice carried wise counsel. Her ready smile reflected a heart for God and His people. Yes, her face, figure, and presentation weren't stylish, but I've never known a more beautiful woman.

Your beauty should not come from outward adornment, such as braided hair and the wearing of gold jewelry and fine clothes. Instead, it should be that of your inner self, the unfading beauty of a gentle and quiet spirit, which is of great worth in God's sight (1 Peter 3:3-4).

In our surface-obsessed culture, let us never forget that the heart is what matters.

Father God, *teach me the meekness and quietness of spirit that will let me reflect You to all who see me. Give me the blessing of serving Your people. In Jesus' most precious name. Amen.*

How Do You Know You Can't Unless You Try?

You never said "I can't" to my grandmother. She always challenged you to try. In fact, trying and failing was preferable to not trying at all. Sometimes the effort required in trying and failing taught you something more valuable than succeeding would have.

When God sets a challenge before you, He expects you to tackle it. There are consequences for not trying, for not following His plans. Look at the children of Israel as they approached the Promised Land. God told Moses to send a leader of every tribe on a reconnaissance mission into Canaan. The purpose was to see the lie of the land and scout out the cities and resources. But when the 12 men came back, 10 of them said the Israelites shouldn't go into the land to possess it because the people were too strong to be overcome. What they didn't reckon into the equation was the Lord's strength and will that would have been with them. Caleb and Joshua, however, believed God and recommended going into the land as God had commanded.

> Caleb silenced the people before Moses and said, "We should go up and take possession of the land, for we can certainly do it." But the men who had gone up with him said, "We can't attack those people; they are stronger than we are" (Numbers 13:30-31).

God's purpose was not thwarted by their disobedience; it was merely delayed. God put off the Israelites' entry into the Promised Land for 40 years, until all those in that generation except Caleb and Joshua were dead. They lost out on experiencing the Promised Land because of their doubt of God's power and might.

Father God, *grant me the courage to try everything You put on my heart to do. Let me believe and depend on Your Word that says I can do all things in You. In Jesus' most precious name. Amen.*

If I Had Meant Baste, I'd Have Said Baste

My grandma was a quilter. She quilted by hand, 10 to 12 stitches to the inch. No machines for her! She loved quilting with friends, but most of them never knew that after they had gone, she unstitched the coarser work and restitched it to her exacting standards. When she was trying to teach me to quilt, she looked at my large stitches and said, "If I had meant baste, I'd have said baste." Then she patiently showed me how to rock the needle in the fine motion she used to get her stitches.

Whatever she undertook, the quality of her work had to be exemplary. "If it is worth doing, it is worth doing well," she declared.

So whether you eat or drink or whatever you do,
do it all for the glory of God (1 Corinthians 10:31).

If we remember that whatever we do reflects on the body of Christ, we need to take care that we do all things diligently and to the best of our abilities. That does not mean we shouldn't attempt to do things simply because we aren't great at that particular activity. It means that when we try something new, we need to pay attention so we can become better at it as we go along. Christians are to always strive for excellence, remembering that all we do (or say or are) reflects on our God.

Father God, help me be deliberate in striving for excellence in all I do this day. In Jesus' most precious name. Amen.

If You Will Dance,
You Must Pay the Piper

Pleasure comes at a price. In my grandma's house, you worked before you stopped for pleasure, effectively paying the piper *before* the dance. Some pleasures crossed the line into the disapproved realm, however. Those were generally indulged in secret and paid for after the fact. For instance, staying up late didn't exempt me from morning chores, no matter how little I had slept. Well do I remember reading late, using a flashlight under the covers, and then having to struggle sleepily through morning chores.

Society tempts us with all kinds of dances. Entertainment and gossip have created an entire industry. Television and movies lure us into spending time passively watching, and some of the viewing offerings are snares to our spirits.

> She sits at the door of her house, on a seat at the highest point of the city, calling out to those who pass by, who go straight on their way. "Let all who are simple come in here!" she says to those who lack judgment. *"Stolen water is sweet; food eaten in secret is delicious!" But little do they know that the dead are there, that her guests are in the depths of the grave* (Proverbs 9:14-18).

When we engage in useless inactivity, we squander time to learn the worthwhile and do the will of God. We forfeit time with Him for the momentary pleasure of the sensational and lurid. We pay the piper in lost opportunities and falling short of our goals.

Father God, *help me know when to dance and when to refrain from dancing. Keep me focused on Your plans for me. In Jesus' most precious name. Amen.*

If Your Head Won't Work, Your Heels Must

Generally my grandma said, "If your head won't work, your heels must" when I had forgotten one of the two items I'd been asked to fetch from one room in the house to another. It meant making a second trip simply because I hadn't thought beyond a single action. But there is a larger context. Luke 14:28-30 says,

> Suppose one of you wants to build a tower. Will he not first sit down and estimate the cost to see if he has enough money to complete it? For if he lays the foundation and is not able to finish it, everyone who sees it will ridicule him, saying, "This fellow began to build and was not able to finish."

Looking toward the completion of a project changes our perspective. Many things need to mesh and come together at the same time. Because every action carries within itself the seed of its own reward or punishment, we must look beyond the single action to the possible results. Sometimes, in frustration, I've said, "Why is there never time to do it right but always enough time to do it over?"

When your head works, you look at the end of the matter and how it functions when it's finished correctly. When your head doesn't work, you find yourself forsaking excellence and having to redo parts of the project simply to make it adequate.

Father God, *grant me the vision to see today from Your eternal perspective. In Jesus' most precious name. Amen.*

Lay All Your Cards on the Table

My grandmother enjoyed playing bridge and pinochle as social recreation. When playing pinochle, Grandma and her friends played in teams, two on each side. Before the play began, they laid portions of their cards on the table in specific configurations for points. This was called "the meld." Your partner then knew some of what was in your hand—and so did your opponents. But some of the cards weren't shown, so the entire truth of your hand wasn't on display. So part of the game involved subterfuge—to play the cards in such a way that your team would win most of the "tricks."

"Laying all your cards on the table" means holding nothing back. This is a definition of honesty. When you're the same person on the outside as you are on the inside, you have achieved a major goal in spiritual growth.

> Surely you desire truth in the inner parts; you teach me wisdom in the inmost place (Psalm 51:6).

Truth in the inner parts becomes integrity for the whole person. The one who loves truth will not countenance or be party to subterfuge. He or she effectively lays all the cards on the table. This openness is the way Christ dealt with everyone He encountered while on earth. Whether offering compassion or rebuke, He never held back on the truth. All His cards were on the table even though some of them could not be understood. If our goal is to be more Christlike, we need to lay our cards on the table as well.

Father God, *imbue me so fully with Your truth that I am unwilling and unable to reflect anything else. Grant me the grace to deal lovingly and truthfully with everyone around me. In Jesus' most precious name. Amen.*

Living High on the Hog

My grandmother used "living high on the hog" to describe someone who was living well, at least in physical terms. The people ate out a lot, dressed well, drove expensive cars, and generally lived "better than most." There was the implication that living this way was not to be desired because it often foreshadowed a comedown.

Becoming proud and complacent is so easy when things are going well. And we often feel we deserve the good things that come our way. After all, if we work hard, why shouldn't we reap the benefits? This is dangerous arrogance. Anything good that comes our way is from God. We didn't earn it; we can't expect it. And we certainly shouldn't be miffed if it doesn't come. We only reap the ultimate benefits when we remember *God is the source of all our supply* and we thank Him. If we have the power to earn things in this life, God gave us that power. If good things come our way seemingly by chance, they were directed by God. In fact, living high on the hog can lull us into a sense of self-sufficiency instead of dependency on God.

Remember the LORD your God, for it is he who gives you the ability to produce wealth, and so confirms his covenant, which he swore to your forefathers, as it is today (Deuteronomy 8:18).

When we are living well, it is because of God. Remember to thank Him daily for *all* His gifts, including our ability to earn our bread and help others.

Father God, *help me retain an attitude of gratitude, especially when things in this life are going well for me. Keep me ever mindful of my total dependence on You. In Jesus' most precious name. Amen.*

Make Hay While the Sun Shines

Sloth wasn't tolerated in my grandmother's house. That didn't mean there were no leisure pursuits, but there was no laziness either. "Relaxing" activities were the creative things Grandma did: knitting, crocheting, hardanger embroidery (a technique from Norway), reading, studying photography, sketching, and china painting. There was no hedonism about her recreation. It was always creative.

We generally can't say the same about ourselves today. Our leisure doesn't always result in something creative. Sometimes—much too often in fact—our choices of activities often titillate the flesh. Today's entertainment seems to pander to celebrity and sensationalism without regard to moral standards or ethical concerns. We need to remember that what doesn't edify dissipates, and what doesn't build up adds to decay and destruction.

> Be very careful, then, how you live—not as unwise but as wise, making the most of every opportunity, because the days are evil (Ephesians 5:15-16).

So many people today are focused on themselves and how to find their own happiness and pleasure. As Christians we are to use our time wisely, expending our efforts toward creative endeavors, whether it be handwork, culinary excellence, or keeping a spotless house so we will draw people to Jesus. There are many ways to be creative in making a beautiful and serene haven in our corner of the world. The fulfillment that comes from a finished creation for God's glory is much more satisfying than simply being entertained with the sensational.

Father God, show me my creative bent so I can redeem my leisure time with recreation that refreshes me and the people around me. In Jesus' most precious name. Amen.

Make Your Words Sweet and Tender

Harsh words and loud voices were unknown in my grandmother's house. I only heard her raise her voice once—when my grandfather dropped the ceiling light in the kitchen, scattering fluorescent tube fragments all over the floor. Even then it was a short burst, and immediately her voice was back to its modulated timbre.

In Grandma's home you could voice anger, excitement, and surprise, but you always held your emotions in check. Her frequent admonition was, "Make your words sweet and tender. You never know when you may have to eat them."

Since I have had to chew and swallow some really tough crow in my life, I appreciate that admonition more than ever. Anticipating the effects of my words *before* letting them escape my lips has saved me much grief. Not anticipating them has caused me great sorrow. Being slow of speech is not a failing but a saving grace.

Everyone should be quick to listen, slow to speak and slow to become angry, for man's anger does not bring about the righteous life that God desires (James 1:19-20).

Unfortunately most of my anger is not the righteous anger of God but the petty anger of self. It arises when something I feel is my due has been withheld or violated. Nothing, however, is my due. Everything is God's to bestow or withhold. And He has my best interest at heart.

Father God, help me bridle my tongue, open my ears, and sweeten my voice that I may better reflect Your grace and love to this world. In Jesus' most precious name. Amen.

Marry in Haste; Repent at Leisure

When I attained enough years to go out with boys, my grandmother was full of cautions. She knew all about the hormones of youth and the accompanying pitfalls. She also knew that "marry in haste; repent at leisure" had a wider application than just weddings.

Making any large decision in haste can have unwelcome consequences. In fact, Grandma recommended seeking the counsel of others when faced with important choices. Besides marriage, what important decisions do we make? Do we go to all our classes when we're in school? Do we stay within our financial budget? Do we invest in furniture for a home? Will we pursue specific careers? What do we do when something we planned on doesn't turn out as expected?

Plans fail for lack of counsel, but with many advisers they succeed (Proverbs 15:22).

Of course, we need to seek the counsel of *qualified* individuals. The first qualification being that the person whose counsel you are seeking loves the Lord and lives by His principles. The second important factor is that the person has your best interest at heart. Next make sure the person has knowledge, experience, and wisdom in the area for which you are seeking help. These can be difficult qualifications to meet. There is, however, one unfailing source of such counsel. You will find it in prayer. God has your best interests at heart. He has all wisdom and knowledge. Seek His counsel first. Others may confirm your hearing of that counsel, but shun any counsel that doesn't resonate first in talking to God.

Father God, *remind me to seek You first in all things. You give wisdom to those who ask of You. Grant me the foresight to seek Your wisdom first, not last. In Jesus' most precious name. Amen.*

Mind Your P's and Q's

I never knew where my grandmother learned this phrase, nor did I ever ask what P's and Q's stood for. It simply meant that in polite company I was to be respectful and be careful not to spill anything or soil my dress so I wouldn't embarrass her or the family. Grandma took every opportunity to teach me, which she did mostly by example. She allowed me to participate in whatever chores or activities she was doing. We never seemed to have time on our hands. There was always something to do, something to learn.

Teaching children is the most important job a parent can have. It isn't one that can be farmed out to someone else. Only you can teach your children your values and the things that are important to you. God wants to teach His children as well. Several times in Scripture He gathers the nation of Israel together to have the word of the law read out loud:

> When all Israel comes to appear before the LORD your God at the place he will choose, you shall read this law before them in their hearing. Assemble the people—men, women and children, and the aliens living in your towns—so they can listen and learn to fear the LORD your God and follow carefully all the words of this law. Their children, who do not know this law, must hear it and learn to fear the LORD your God as long as you live in the land you are crossing the Jordan to possess (Deuteronomy 31:11-13).

He is telling the children of Israel to be careful of their behavior so it will reflect well on their God.

Father God, *remind me often of what You want me to be in this world. Keep me close to Your guiding hand so I will reflect only Your values to the people around me. In Jesus' most precious name. Amen.*

The Nearest Helping Hand
Is at the End of Your Arm

My grandmother didn't put up with whining and complaining. If you wanted something done, she taught you how to do it yourself. She was not a servant in her house, although she did have a serving heart. Her service was given voluntarily, not at someone's whim or demand.

By not doing things for me, she taught me many skills that have been very valuable. First I learned that you can't always have someone at your beck and call. Second, I learned that you can always learn new skills and crafts. Third, I discovered the satisfaction of completing a job without relying on someone else.

Over the years I've had cause many times to bless Grandma for this gift of "do it yourself." Being able to do things means that when something needs to be done, I can do it without waiting for someone else to have the time. Yes, there are certain things I can't do. Changing a lightbulb in the house is a simple chore, but rewiring the kitchen requires a professional. And there is wisdom in knowing the difference.

Make it your ambition to lead a quiet life, to mind your own business and to work with your hands, just as we told you, so that your daily life may win the respect of outsiders and so that you will not be dependent on anybody (1 Thessalonians 4:11-12).

Although our identity in Christ focuses on our relationship, not our accomplishments, we are told to be doers of the Word, not hearers only. What we do reflects on who we are and Whose we are.

Father God, *help me be capable of all the tasks You ask of me. Give me a heart for diligent labor so I will never disgrace You. In Jesus' most precious name. Amen.*

Never Judge a Book by Its Cover

To some extent, we all judge by appearances. For instance, publishers today take great pains to make their book covers attractive to readers. But that wasn't always the case. Antique books are frequently a simple cloth binding with the title and author's name imprinted on the exterior. The books had to be judged by the content inside.

While browsing in the city library where my grandmother worked, I found that the plainest exterior could hide wonderful works, such as Shakespeare's plays, Robert Burns' poetry, Honoré de Balzac's bawdy stories, and the truths of the Bible.

People are much like books. The most ordinary exterior can contain anything from a heart filled with love for God to the malicious evil of a Mephistopheles...and everything in between. Seeing with earthly eyes, we can be fooled by appearances. We need the discernment of the Lord to see the hearts within.

The Lord sent Samuel to anoint Saul's successor to the throne of Israel. When God's prophet, Samuel, first saw the handsome Eliab he thought surely he was the one God had chosen:

> But the LORD said to Samuel, "Do not consider his appearance or his height, for I have rejected him. The Lord does not look at the things man looks at. Man looks at the outward appearance, but the LORD looks at the heart" (1 Samuel 16:7).

God's chosen was not even among the brothers presented to Samuel. No, David was in the field tending sheep and had to be summoned. He was the least likely candidate, being but a boy.

Father God, *keep me from judging by appearances alone. Grant me the grace to see the hearts within before deciding about others. In Jesus' most precious name. Amen.*

Never Put Off to Tomorrow What You Can Do Today

Procrastination is a sneaky thief that will rob us of our accomplishments if we let it. Have you heard the cautionary tale told about the devil's council? Suggestions were being taken regarding getting people into his domain. One demon suggested telling people there was no God. Another suggested convincing them there was no hell. But the suggestion that received the widest approval was telling them that God was real and so was hell, but there was no hurry to follow God because there would be plenty of time to worry about that later.

The most precious commodity we have is time. Once gone, it can never be recovered. Spent foolishly, we become poorer. But if we spend our time wisely, profitably, and in the service of God, we lay up for ourselves treasures in heaven. In that sense, today is all there is. This moment is the only moment we have. We can be gone in an instant, in the twinkling of an eye. We are not promised any specific time allotment on this earth. We can't count on tomorrow or next week or next year.

> God said to him, "You fool! This very night your life will be demanded from you" (Luke 12:20).

If you knew that you had only one year to live, what would you do with it? How would you spend that time? If it were only a month, or a week, or a day, would that change how you spend your time? Resolve to live in light of your answer.

Father God, give me the wisdom to use the time You've given me wisely and in Your service. Keep me focused on the eternal and undistracted by the temporary. In Jesus' most precious name. Amen.

One Good Turn Deserves Another

My grandma never forgot a favor done for her. She always tried to repay kindness with another kindness, and she instilled in us the virtue of a grateful heart. In this she was following a great biblical example. David and Jonathan were friends—they were the very definition of friends. Jonathan had many reasons to be jealous of David. After all, Jonathan was the son of Saul, the current king, but David had been anointed to succeed Saul as king. Far from being jealous, Jonathan loved David and showed him every kindness, even helping him escape from Saul's wrath:

> Jonathan was very fond of David and warned him, "My father Saul is looking for a chance to kill you. Be on your guard tomorrow morning; go into hiding and stay there. I will go out and stand with my father in the field where you are. I'll speak to him about you and will tell you what I find out"
> (1 Samuel 19:1-3).

After the deaths of Saul and Jonathan, David sought out anyone who might be of that house to continue the bonds of love:

> David asked, "Is there anyone still left of the house of Saul to whom I can show kindness for Jonathan's sake?" (2 Samuel 9:1).

Then David restored the properties of Saul to Jonathan's son, Mephibosheth, who lived the remainder of his life in the palace with David as if he were David's son. This was not a simple pie at the door or note of thanks in the mailbox. This was a long-term commitment. Are we as committed to repaying kindness for kindness?

Father God, *instill in me a heart of gratitude and a sensitivity to those who do good to me. I want to be faithful in repaying good deeds in kind. In Jesus' most precious name. Amen.*

Prepare the Distaff and the Spindle, and the Lord Will Provide the Flax

Distaffs and spindles are spinning tools. The distaff is a wooden peg that the spinner uses to wrap the fibrous interior of flax plants around. The spindle is a weight that drawn, or spun, linen thread is wound around when it is finished. The work of actually turning the flax fiber into linen thread takes place between the distaff and the spindle as the spinner's hands work the raw flax into a long, continuous twisted strand of linen thread.

In the Christian life, the distaff—our support—is the Word of God. We need to know it well. The spindle is anything that puts stress on our lives. And the flax is the people we interact with or have influence with. When we have assimilated the Word of God and strengthened our hands through the stresses that have come upon us, we are prepared to work with and help people so they will want to know God and, hopefully, become part of the Christian family.

> In your hearts set apart Christ as Lord. Always be prepared to give an answer to everyone who asks you to give the reason for the hope that you have. But do this with gentleness and respect (1 Peter 3:15).

We may not think of ourselves as evangelists, but *every follower of Christ* is heir to the Savior's great commission. If we know who God is and what He has done for us, if we can explain the effects of God in our lives, we can win souls for Christ.

Father God, *teach me and strengthen my hands so that I may add precious threads to the tapestry You are weaving in my life and in the lives of the people around me. In Jesus' most precious name. Amen.*

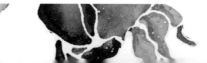

Pretty Is as Pretty Does

My grandmother was unimpressed with my attempts to be pretty. Clothes, hairstyles, makeup, and jewelry underwent her close inspection. But even when they were approved as satisfactory, she always cautioned, "Pretty is as pretty does."

While outward appearances were important to a degree, she expected my actions to equal or surpass mere outward adornments. Those expectations included devotion to daily duty and generosity to others.

> In her hand she holds the distaff and grasps the spindle with her fingers. She opens her arms to the poor and extends her hands to the needy (Proverbs 31:19-20).

By my grandmother's definition, the Proverbs 31 woman was truly pretty. She was busy at the work of her household and generous to those less fortunate. She had mastered the balance of duty and charitable generosity.

Sometimes we are so caught up in the busyness of our lives that we fail to see the needs of the people around us. We worry about dress sizes or crow's feet around the eyes when we should be more concerned with our ability to see someone else's heartaches so we can reach out to them. Conversely, we might be so caught up in the needs and wants of others that our homes and families are short-changed. We need to learn to strike the same balance as the Proverbs 31 woman, who tended the needs of her household and was still generous to others.

Father God, help me learn the balance between family responsibilities and community needs. Keep me faithful to You in all my endeavors. In Jesus' most precious name. Amen.

Strike While the Iron Is Hot

If you have ever watched a blacksmith at the forge, you've seen him plunge the iron into a hot flame. The dark metal fires to a yellow orange. Then he moves the iron from the fire to the anvil and hammers it into the desired shape. The iron darkens as it cools. While the iron is hot, it is malleable and can be shaped any way the smith desires. Because shaping takes time, the iron cools and must be reheated multiple times before he is satisfied with his work. At that point he plunges the iron into a bucket of water to cool it quickly, making the iron firm again. After it has cooled, the shape is permanent unless it's reheated again.

The skill of the smith lies in knowing the readiness of the material by its color in the flame and his ability to work the metal when it is ready. Timing is everything. If he doesn't work quickly, he loses the heat and the iron must go back into the fire. How does this relate to our Christian walk? We must always be ready and available to reach out to help others:

> As we have opportunity, let us do good to all people, especially to those who belong to the family of believers (Galatians 6:10).

Opportunity is as fleeting as the heat in iron. Our readiness to move when opportunity is available can make an enormous difference in our lives and in the lives of others.

Father God, *still my heart to hear Your voice and strengthen my hands to do service in Your name. In Jesus' most precious name. Amen.*

Success Consists of Getting Up One More Time Than You Fall Down

My grandmother never hesitated to try new things. She never seemed to be afraid of failure. Each time something didn't work well, she devised another method of accomplishing the same thing or she went on to something new. Not succeeding didn't discourage her.

Failure is a built-in feature of growth. We learn from it what will not work. Even when Jesus sent the disciples forth to teach and heal, He set a parameter for dealing with failure:

> Calling the Twelve to him, he sent them out two by two and gave them authority over evil spirits. These were his instructions: "Take nothing for the journey except a staff—no bread, no bag, no money in your belts. Wear sandals but not an extra tunic. Whenever you enter a house, stay there until you leave that town. And if any place will not welcome you or listen to you, shake the dust off your feet when you leave, as a testimony against them" (Mark 6:7-11).

In sending the disciples, Jesus knew they would not be successful in all places, at all times. He commanded that they "shake the dust off your feet when you leave." They were not to carry the remnants of that failure into the next city.

As we've noted, we learn from our failures what not to do. As long as we remember that, we can move confidently to the next project because we know how to get up again.

Father God, *remind me that You are with me even when I fall short. Grant me the grace to rely upon You in all things and to keep moving forward in Your will. In Jesus' most precious name. Amen.*

Those Who Can, Do, and Those Who Can't, Come Late and Criticize

My grandmother dismissed much criticism by saying, "Those who can, do, and those who can't, come late and criticize." Constructive critique was always welcome, but when people criticized for the sake of feeling important, she simply disregarded their words. During the years she painted china with a small group of friends, I watched her handle criticism. If Irma suggested that she pat the background with a silk-wrapped cotton ball rather than a sponge, this was valuable criticism. It was designed to *assist* her effort and provide a favorable result. If someone said she couldn't paint a pansy a specific shade of purple, she thought a moment, and then chose to heed or disregard that opinion. I have come to appreciate this mind-set more and more.

So often it seems people want to tear down others, not build them up. When you hear criticism, remember you're in good company. Moses put up with a lot of criticism and complaining from the children of Israel during the exodus from Egypt:

> [The people] spoke against God and against Moses, and said, "Why have you brought us up out of Egypt to die in the desert? There is no bread! There is no water! And we detest this miserable food!" (Numbers 21:5).

The Israelites had ample evidence of God's provision for them. They were eating manna and complaining about it. Their need was met, but not their desires. And as long as someone else was responsible for doing, they felt free to complain. I realize that sometimes I need to examine myself, asking, "Am I the doer or the complainer?" How about you?

Father God, *help me be a doer, not a complainer, in Your kingdom. Turn my eyes toward the needs at hand and not the lusts of my heart and flesh. In Jesus' most precious name. Amen.*

Time and Tide Wait for No Man

My grandmother insisted on punctuality. If you were to leave for an event at two o'clock, she insisted that you be dressed and ready by half past one. By a quarter of two, your purse and coat, if needed, were laid on the arm of the chair next to the door if someone was coming to pick you up. If you were going on your own and had a ten-minute drive, you left at one-forty. Being late was unthinkable because it showed disrespect for the other people involved in the occasion.

I have struggled with punctuality all my life. There always seems to be just one more thing to be done before I can be ready to go. I'm still learning to master this wisdom. Thinking of the pace at which time slips through my fingers, I feel a sense of urgency. There are things to be done that will not wait. And I certainly don't want to be telling the Lord that it didn't get done because I didn't apply myself to the task.

> Teach us to number our days aright, that we may gain a heart of wisdom (Psalm 90:12).

Our days are numbered, from the first breath to the last. God knows the end before we have even begun, but that is generally His secret. He doesn't disclose the end to us before we need to know it. In the meantime we have work to do—His work.

Father God, *make me aware of the gift of time. Help me appreciate how You want me to use the time You have given me. Prod me so I won't be an idler. In Jesus' most precious name. Amen.*

Turn the Corners of Your Mouth a Little Upwards, Don't You Know

Pouting was unacceptable in my grandmother's presence. She always wore a pleasant expression and expected the same of you. She learned this little poem at her mother's knee:

Turn the corners of your mouth
A little upwards, don't you know.
If you keep a-smiling always,
Discontent ain't room to grow.

And Grandma repeated this frequently to those of us inclined to pout and be unhappy. When she teased the corner of our mouths upward with a gentle finger, it was hard to keep frowning.

Our response to life isn't so much a reaction to the things that happen as it is a product of what we tell ourselves about the things that happen. If we dwell on all the negatives in our lives, we will always be unhappy. If we think about the things that have gone right, we will smile.

> Whatever is true, whatever is noble, whatever is right, whatever is pure, whatever is lovely, whatever is admirable—if anything is excellent or praiseworthy—think about such things (Philippians 4:8).

The trick is to find the things that are admirable and praiseworthy. Sometimes we need to hunt for them, especially if we're looking for earthly things. There is one thing that is true and pure, however—God's love for us. And He promises to never forsake those who put their trust in Him. That should put an eternal smile on all our faces!

Father God, *when the world seems negative and dark, remind me that You are as near as my next breath and that Your love for me never fails. In Jesus' most precious name. Amen.*

Where There Is a Will, There Is a Way

Difficulties were merely challenges in my grandmother's vocabulary. If something needed to be done, there had to be a way to do it. She often said, "Where there is a will, there is a way," adding that if you wanted something badly enough you'd find a way to make it happen. In that, she was only partially right. In the intervening years, I've discovered that if it is in God's will, *He will make it happen.* Our part is to be obedient and not stand in God's way. We don't want to limit His work in our lives by our unbelief. Even Jesus didn't do mighty works in Nazareth because the people there couldn't get beyond his being "the carpenter's son" (Matthew 13:54-58).

While looking to accomplish those things we desire, we need to be certain they comply with God's will. If a door we want to go through seems securely closed, we need to test whether He has closed it. How do we do this? By asking Him! We can pray and ask God. And if He didn't close the door, we can ask for His help in getting it open. Jesus said,

> What is impossible with men is possible with God (Luke 18:27).

Our God is able to do all things and to empower us to do the same in His name. Our part is to believe He can—and will—guide and help us.

Father God, help me remember that You are bigger than all the obstacles in this world. Remind me to stay close to You so I will never be out of Your will. In Jesus' most precious name. Amen.

Who Said Life Was Fair?

My grandmother had no illusions about life being fair. She had weathered her share of hardships and troubles. She knew poverty firsthand, reared a family, sent sons to war, and buried a grandbaby. Many of the women of her generation experienced the same storms.

Behind the faces we see every day, there are stories about unfairness. If we knew some of those stories, we might be more patient with what we see as faults or shortcomings in others. This world, no longer a Garden of Eden, is an imperfect place that includes cruelty, disaster, disease, and failure. We all face these things, but we *are not* slaves to them. What did Jesus tell His disciples about unfairness?

> I have told you these things, so that in me you may have peace. In this world you will have trouble. But take heart! I have overcome the world (John 16:33).

Jesus wanted them to know that this world is *not* the end. We have a place in heaven where we will not be subject to tribulation. But there is no fairness there either. We are given preferential treatment under the blood of Christ. We will not get what we deserve. We will get what Christ has reserved for us: His peace and His favor. In that light, fairness seems highly overrated, doesn't it?

Father God, open my eyes to Your justice and standards. Deliver me from the pettiness of my human standards of fairness. Plant gratitude in my heart. In Jesus' most precious name. Amen.

You Can Always Do Just One More Thing

My grandmother's energy never ceased to amaze me. She was active and doing new things far into her last illness. She lived by the motto that you can always do just one more thing. Her habit of doing one more thing kept her house in good order and enabled her to complete her many creative projects.

As Christians we seem to have a long list of things to do. Families, homes, jobs, civic organizations, and church commitments clamor for our time and attention. The demands seem to multiply like mosquitoes in brackish backwater. Sometimes I think that one more thing is simply not possible. But it is if I modify the saying a bit and think of it as "just one thing more."

> Let us not become weary in doing good, for at the proper time we will reap a harvest if we do not give up (Galatians 6:9).

We are enjoined to keep doing because there is a reward at the end of the doing. That reward *is not* salvation and eternity with God. We have that by just believing and accepting Jesus Christ as our Lord and Savior. Our deeds will be rewarded with crowns—crowns we can lay at Jesus' feet in heaven. Thinking of that crown of reward in eternity spurs me to "not become weary in doing good." My weariness is nothing compared to the joy I will feel in having something to offer the Lord.

Father God, *strengthen my hands and my will to do the additional tasks You want me to accomplish. Remind me of the promised reward—something to offer You when I get to heaven. In Jesus' most precious name. Amen.*

You Can't Stub Your Toe Unless You Are Moving Forward

My grandmother's answer to any failure or setback was "You can't stub your toe unless you are moving forward." Think about it. Physically you can't stub your toe if you are sitting or standing still. It's only when you move that your foot is at risk. And if you don't move that foot, you will never get anywhere.

God has planned for our missteps. He knows we are not perfect and that we learn from our mistakes. He gives us permission to fail, and we have His assurance that failure need not be permanent:

> If the LORD delights in a man's way, he makes his steps firm; though he stumble, he will not fall, for the LORD upholds him with his hand (Psalm 37:23-24).

Moving forward in the face of adversity or challenge is not bravado. It is the courage of our faith in the Lord. He is bigger than our failures and mistakes. He lifts us when we fall. We can, however, keep from falling so often if we consult Him *before* we move: "[The LORD] makes his steps firm." This assurance is in the Word of God for our assurance. Between study of the Bible and time alone with God in prayer, we can be confident that our steps are ordered by the Lord. And when (not if) we stub our toes occasionally, He will help us back up and onto the appointed path.

Father God, grant me the determination to remain solidly grounded in Your Word, no matter the distractions of daily life. Keep me faithful on the path You have set before me. In Jesus' most precious name. Amen.

You Catch More Flies with Honey Than with Vinegar

Rudeness and crudity of language were never tolerated in my grandmother's presence. She believed that you could be polite and pleasant even in a heated discussion. She also believed it served your debate well if you remained pleasant and nonaggressive even when you disagreed vehemently. In order to persuade people to your way of thinking, she believed you needed to lead them gently, not beat them with a stick.

An added benefit to keeping your words sweet is that you have to master your feelings *before* you speak. When you let your emotions take over, you have little control over yourself, your words, the reactions of others. And the negative physiological effects of uncontrolled anger are well-documented: elevated blood pressure and the increased possibility of heart attack or stroke.

> Pleasant words are a honeycomb, sweet to the soul and healing to the bones (Proverbs 16:24).

To maintain control in times of great stress I follow a pattern. First, I remind myself that nothing has happened without God's permission and provision. Second, I remember that God loves me and has my best interests at heart. Third, I tell myself there is a lesson somewhere in this circumstance, and it's my job to find it for my benefit and, perhaps, disseminate it to others. In doing this, perhaps I can draw others into the saving knowledge of Christ. And if the truth I need to tell is difficult, perhaps it will be heard more clearly if the words I use are soft and sweet.

Father God, *help me keep honey on my tongue—not the honey of insincere flattery, but the wholesome honey of Your Word and love. In Jesus' most precious name. Amen.*

You Will Be Polite to Company

Hospitality was the rule in my grandma's house. She knew how to entertain royally on a frugal budget. Guests were always expected and welcomed after ten o'clock in the morning. By that time, people should have all their daily chores out of the way and be moving on to other activities. Grandma occupied her "leisure" time with reading and textile arts that could be quickly and easily laid aside should someone come to the door.

When I balked at participating in the entertaining because the company wasn't someone I cared about, her admonition was always, "I don't care how you feel about it. You will put on a pretty face and come downstairs and be polite to the company." And when she said "pretty face" she was referring to maintaining a pleasant disposition and a ready smile.

Let your conversation be always full of grace, seasoned with salt, so that you may know how to answer everyone (Colossians 4:6).

"Evangelism" is a scary word to some of us. However, if we remember that everyone is to be invited to the wedding feast of Christ, we might think more about how we approach people—or rather how to get them to approach us. If we are smiling, welcoming, and open, people will be drawn to us. Then we can share with them the hope that is within us.

Father God, help me be welcoming and gracious to everyone in this hurting world so they will listen when I share about You and come to the wedding feast of the Lamb. In Jesus' most precious name. Amen.

You Will Not Make a Scene and Disgrace the Family

One of my grandma's cardinal rules was that no matter the circumstance you never made a scene. Temper tantrums were unheard of in her household. In the first place, they were ineffective. In the second, they brought unwelcome consequences. The injunction held true in all cases, whether it was a funeral or a party. You maintained your composure and ladylike bearing. I was glad for this training when tragedies happened in our family later because I was able to cope better.

For instance, when my uncle was murdered at work, my mother and I attended every court session held for the people arrested for the crime. We didn't speak to the media because law enforcement asked us not to. After one particularly trying day, a local reporter stopped us in the courthouse hall and asked, "Off the record, I've watched you two in court day after day, and you seem so calm and composed. How do you do it?"

We looked at each other and laughed quietly. We'd been trained so thoroughly in stoicism that there was never a question that we wouldn't be composed in public.

> In everything set them an example by doing what is good. In your teaching show integrity, seriousness and soundness of speech that cannot be condemned, so that those who oppose you may be ashamed because they have nothing bad to say about us (Titus 2:7-8).

We need to be aware as Christians that people are watching us. They look for inconsistencies in our Christian walk. Can we really say that all we do is reflecting well on Christ?

Father God, keep me aware of the impression I leave with others. Let me reflect You in all I do and say. In Jesus' most precious name. Amen.

You'll Never Learn Any Younger

Until the day she entered the hospital during her last illness, my grandmother kept learning new things, discovering new crafts, and coming up with new ideas. When I was curious about something, she didn't give me the answers. She sent me to the dictionary or the encyclopedia to look up the topic. Her formal education ended at the fourth grade, but she was wise and well-read. It never bothered her that other people, younger than she, knew things she didn't. If she was curious, she set herself to learning about it. Doing so, she learned more than many people with advanced degrees.

> If you call out for insight and cry aloud for understanding, and if you look for it as for silver and search for it as for hidden treasure, then you will understand the fear of the Lord and find the knowledge of God (Proverbs 2:3-5).

We are told to seek knowledge and the wisdom of God. It is the privilege of the Christian to seek this knowledge, not merely for the knowledge itself, but to become more like the One we seek to know better. The source of our knowledge of Him is our time in the Scriptures, our time in worship, and our quiet time with Him. Even if our available time is limited, we can learn something new of God every day.

Father God, *help me prioritize my time and give You the first of it each day. Grant me the ability to focus completely and learn effectively. In Jesus' most precious name. Amen.*